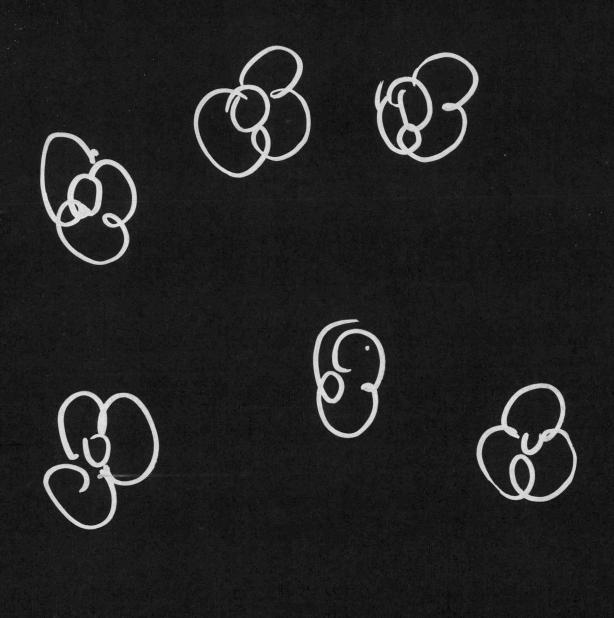

Audrey Hepburn

PULTENEY PRESS

Published by International Book Marketing Ltd
First published in 2009

Pulteney Press
I Riverside Court
St Johns Road
Bath, BA2 6PD, UK

© Atlantic Publishing
For details of picture copyrights see page 96

A catalogue record for this book is available from the British Library.
ISBN: 978-1-906734-57-2

Opposite and left: Audrey Hepburn became one of the great style icons of the twentieth century. She changed the look of the movie star. Early in her career, she refused to conform to the fashion for the more voluptuous figure, never wearing "padding" of any kind. These early studio shots already convey the qualities of innocence and directness that made audiences love and admire her.

Audrey Hepburn was born Audrey Kathleen Ruston in Belgium in 1928 to a Dutch mother and an English father. Her mother, Baroness Ella van Heemstra, was a devoted but undemonstrative woman; her father, Joseph Ruston, abandoned them when Audrey was still a child. She described this as the most "traumatic" event of her life. Audrey attended school in England but moved back to Holland during the war. Under German occupation, she and her mother worked for the Dutch Resistance, coming close to starvation.

Left and oppposite: Audrey pictured in 1950 after the run of the revue *Sauce Piquante* in London's West End in which she was a dancer. "I worked like an idiot!" she remarked of this time. After an early beginning in musical theater, Audrey performed very seldom on stage, preferring films. To subsidize her earnings at the beginning of her career, Audrey began modeling. This gave her an early understanding of her relationship with the camera and a sense of fashion.

Opposite: 1950, in Richmond Park, London.
Audrey had trained with the great dancer Marie
Rambert in London, although she was not
chosen to tour with Rambert's Sadler's Wells
Ballet company. She was considered too tall and
did not have the stamina, probably a result of
the deprivations of the war. However, she never
lost the litheness and poise that sprang from
her early training.

Right: A still from the film *Laughter in Paradise*,
1951. Here she plays a bit part of a cigarette-
seller in a nightclub. Although her part was
minuscule, she was noticed and the studio was
keen to hang on to her.

Opposite: Christmas, 1949; Audrey poses with other members of the cast of the *Sauce Tartare* revue in London. Although Audrey was a low-ranking chorus girl, her colleagues noticed her talent. The musical star Jessie Matthews said, "She just had to be a star given the right breaks." In three years she would have filmed *Roman Holiday*, the movie that earned her an Academy Award.

Right: Audrey modeling a bonnet, 1951. The comedian Bob Monkhouse, who performed in the revue *Sauce Piquante*, said: "Her appearance was so adorable that you held your breath while she smiled and batted her eyes."

Right: Audrey dancing on the set of
Secret People, 1951. This was her first
major role in a film, where the famous
"quality" was noted. Her fellow-actors
Serge Reggiani and Valentina Cortese
impressed her with their reservations
about publicity. Cortese said, "In
Hollywood, it is terrible – they expect
you to be their slave; you have to be
ready to do anything for them, at any
time, not just when you're making a
picture … Liberty is the most
wonderful thing of all." It was
important advice. Forever after
Audrey jealously guarded her private
life from the press.

A studio portrait taken in the early
1950s. When photographer Cecil
Beaton met Audrey he described her
as having "a new type of beauty: huge
mouth, flat Mongolian features … Her
enormous potential cinema success
seems to have made little impression
on this delightful human being."

Left: In 1952 Audrey was engaged to Englishman James Hanson, heir to a business fortune. Audrey was often abroad filming and James led the life of a playboy back at home, often appearing with different glamorous women in the society pages of the papers. Audrey broke off the engagement.

Opposite: Audrey demonstrating that she could carry off with style even the most unlikely headgear. This was taken on a lake in Switzerland, the country in which she lived for most of her adult life.

Opposite: Audrey shows off her putting skills. Gregory Peck said years later of Audrey's talents as a comedienne: "She's a very funny lady … I have always thought that she should have played more comedy … It's not that she hasn't had a great career … but I wish she had been allowed to do a few broad comedies along the way."

Above: A still from *The Lavender Hill Mob*, 1951, in which Audrey played Alec Guinness's girlfriend Chiquita. Audrey calculated how long she appeared on screen in the six films she made during 1950 and 1951: "They made [a total of] one quick appearance."

Opposite: Audrey's astonishing break was to be cast in the lead role in *Roman Holiday*, playing opposite Gregory Peck. She was spotted on the cover of a magazine by a casting director. Paramount Studios and the director of the film, William Wyler, wanted someone relatively unknown for the part. After her screen test, and without Audrey's knowledge, they kept the cameras rolling. She discussed her youth in German-occupied Holland, and displayed an artlessness which Wyler was careful to nurture. Audrey never seemed to be acting.

Above: In 1953 Audrey met Mel Ferrer, an American actor/director/producer, twelve years her senior. She was twenty-four, he was still married to his third wife. From that first meeting they were almost inseparable. And from the very beginning, he was to exert an enormous influence on her career.

Opposite: A publicity shot from *Roman Holiday*, released in 1953. This film defined her screen personality and shot her to stardom and an Academy Award. It also typecast her for many years in the role of ingénue, often playing against older men.

Above: Audrey and her leading man, Gregory Peck, in a street scene in Rome. Audrey loved to film in Europe, where she felt most at home. Peck was a warm and generous co-star. He said that there was "nothing mean or petty [about Audrey] ... she didn't have any of the backstabbing, grasping, petty, gossipy personality that you see in this business. I liked her a lot; in fact I loved her. It was easy to love her."

Above: Audrey on the arm of Harcourt Williams, in her grand entrance in *Roman Holiday*, 1953. Her character is a young princess bored with the daily routine of royal life. She escapes for a night and a day and meets a handsome journalist, played by Gregory Peck, but returns finally to duty. In many ways it is a bittersweet reversal of the Cinderella story.

Opposite: Audrey holding her Oscar for Best Actress for *Roman Holiday*, 1954, with the press literally at her feet.

Right: At Claridge's, London, 1953. Audrey's next role was to be in *Sabrina*, co-starring Humphrey Bogart and William Holden and directed by the great Billy Wilder. Sabrina is the beautiful daughter of a chauffeur to the wealthy Larrabee family who returns from five years in Paris, transformed into a dazzling wit. The two Larrabee brothers, played by Bogart and Holden, compete for her affections.

Opposite: Audrey on the verge of stardom.

Left: A promotional portrait of Audrey for *Sabrina*, 1953. The costume designer for the film was Hubert de Givenchy. Givenchy's and Audrey's names were from then forever linked, as he designed many of the clothes for her films and her personal wardrobe. He also created a perfume for her and when he handed it over, she exclaimed, "*Mais c'est interdit!*" [But it's forbidden!]. He famously named the perfume L'Interdit. Audrey treasured his friendship throughout her life.

Opposite: Audrey and Humphrey Bogart in a publicity shot for *Sabrina*.

Left: Audrey's distinctive looks were matched by her distinctive voice, which some critics found affected. Born in Belgium of a Dutch mother and English father, she spoke French, Dutch and English equally. "There is no speech I can relax into when I'm tired, because my ear has never been accustomed to one intonation. It's because I have no mother tongue that the critics accuse me of curious speech."

Opposite: The chemistry between Audrey and Holden is palpable. They had a very passionate affair during the filming of Sabrina. She may have considered leaving Mel for Holden, who was willing to leave his wife for Audrey. However, when Audrey discovered that Holden could have no more children, she ended their relationship, devastated. It was her dearest wish to have children.

Above: Audrey with Humphrey Bogart on the set of *Sabrina*. Cary Grant, still a youthful fifty, turned down the role that Bogie accepted. Billy Wilder was characteristically witty when asked why Bogart — and not thirty-five-year-old Holden — gets the girl: "Because Bogart gets $300,000 a picture and Holden gets $125,000."

Opposite: The legendary Marlene Dietrich visits Audrey during the shooting of *Sabrina*. Like Dietrich, Audrey remained very much a European actress working in the American film industry.

Opposite: William Holden and Audrey look the lighthearted couple, during the filming of *Sabrina*. Nine years later they worked together again on the underrated *Paris – When It Sizzles*. Holden recalled arriving at Orly airport in Paris to start shooting: "I could hear my footsteps echoing against the walls of the transit corridor, just like a condemned man walking the last mile. I realized that I had to face Audrey and I had to deal with my drinking." He succeeded for a short while but relapsed after a week.

Right: Audrey was plagued with doubts about her own ability. It made her strive to do well, which was always noted by her colleagues. She said, after winning a Tony for playing the title role in the play *Ondine* on Broadway: "I can't allow … all this public acclaim to turn my head."

Opposite: Audrey leaning out of a car window on the set of *Sabrina*.

Right: In England, Audrey, accompanied by Mel, receives her *Picturegoer* award for 1953–54. She had appeared on the cover of this magazine a few years earlier, featured as a rising star. Mel managed much of her career, often using it as a springboard for his own. He co-starred with her in New York in *Ondine* and notoriously overrode the director's instruction for Audrey to take single curtain call.

Opposite and above: Givenchy said of Audrey: "Unlike many of her illustrious colleagues, she did not behave like a spoilt star. She knew exactly how to shape her strong, independent image. This naturally extended to the way she dressed, and so she always took the clothes created for her one step further by adding something of her own – some small personal detail that enhanced the whole."

Left and opposite: The Ferrers married in Bürgenstock, Switzerland on September 24, 1954. Audrey had escaped from New York to Switzerland with Mel and her mother after Ondine finished, close to nervous exhaustion. To reporters in New York she had deflected questions about an impending marriage: "Unless you know your innermost thoughts, you can't give yourself to anyone … That's why I don't want to be tied down to one spot, or even to one man." Her dress was, of course, designed by Givenchy.

Opposite: From her early days as a model, Audrey understood the importance of good lighting and the right angles.

Above: A still from *War and Peace*, with English actor Jeremy Brett, 1956. This adaptation of Tolstoy's novel had a stellar cast and was Hollywood's attempt to serve the public an epic with which television could not compete. The director King Vidor said at the time, "It was of course inconceivable to have anyone other than Audrey Hepburn as Natasha. She has a rhythmic grace that is a director's delight."

Opposite: Audrey's sylphlike figure was unusual, given the style of the day. During the filming of a ballroom sequence in *War and Peace*, the cameraman Jack Cardiff complained that she was too thin for her costume. "I suggested she wear a necklace or something with this low-cut dress, but she said, 'Jack, I'm just me. I am what I am, and I haven't done too badly like this.'"

Right: Sketching on the set of *War and Peace*. At first she resisted the idea of playing Natasha; Mel persuaded her to take the part. He was given the role of Prince Andrei. Her friend and publicist Henry Rogers said: "It was no secret that her marriage to Mel was not a happy one ... She never complained, but I always saw the sadness in her eyes ..." She had suffered a first miscarriage earlier that year.

Opposite. A publicity shot of Audrey as she appeared in *Funny Face* (1956), co-starring Fred Astaire. She

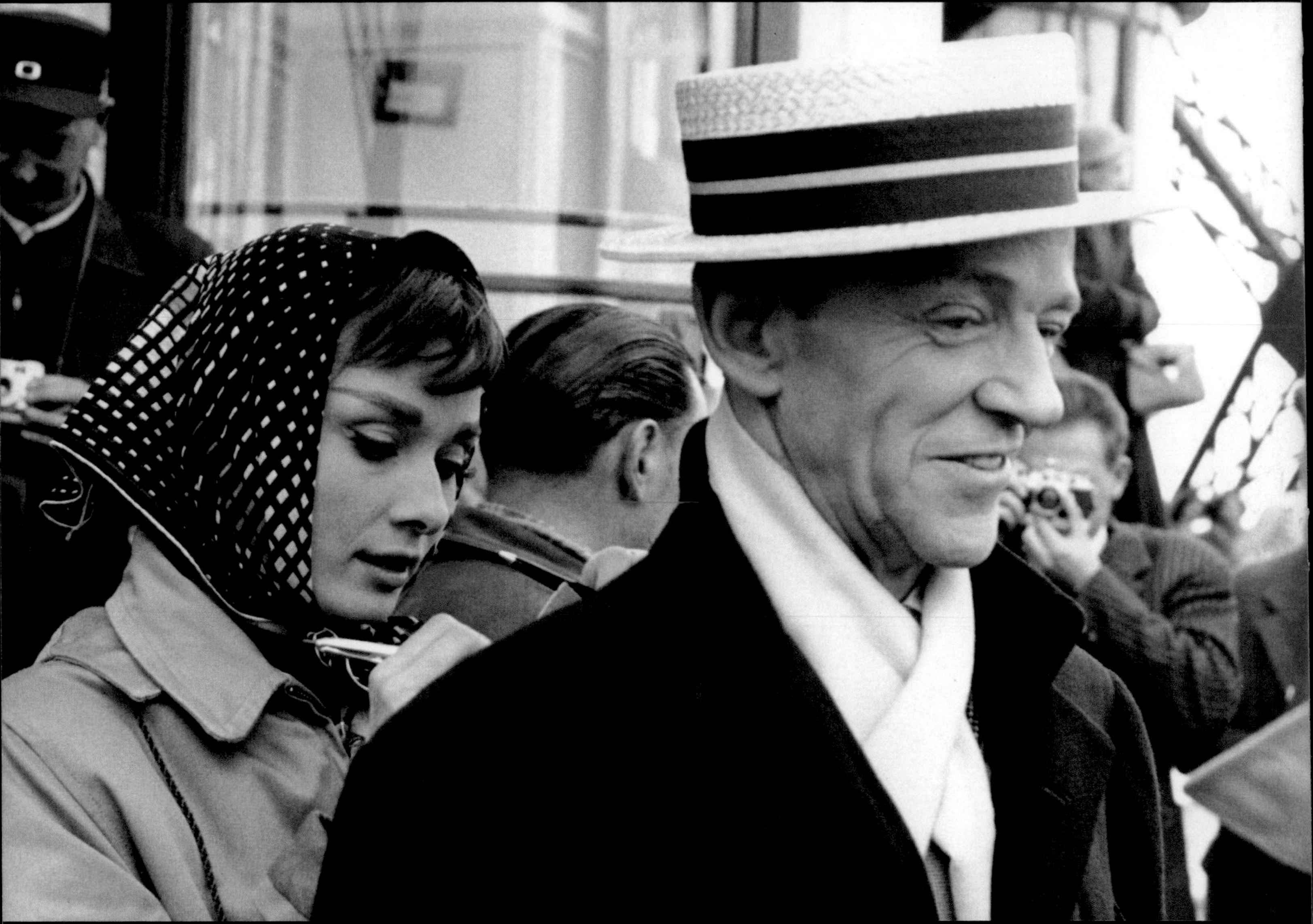

Above: Trying to entertain Gary Cooper in *Love in the Afternoon*, 1956. Yet again Audrey was playing opposite a
man much older than herself. Here she is Ariane, the daughter of a private detective, played by the king of
charm, Maurice Chevalier. Chevalier is investigating Cooper's character, an ageing playboy. Ariane falls for him and
pretends that far from being innocent her young life has been crammed with love affairs.

Opposite: Yet again Audrey proves that she is one of the greatest style icons of the twentieth century, able to
wear a bread basket on her head and brandish a checkered tablecloth with immense panache.

Opposite: A still from *The Nun's Story*, 1959, set and filmed in the Congo. This was, in Audrey's eyes, her greatest and most satisfying role. It was a huge critical and popular success. She was able to draw on her experiences as a teenager working for the Dutch Resistance during the war. While filming she had a passionate affair with Robert Anderson, its scriptwriter.

Right: In 1959 Audrey starred in *Green Mansions*. It was the only time Mel Ferrer directed his wife. The film was not a great success at the box office, and luckily for Audrey, the release of *The Nun's Story* followed quickly and eclipsed it.

Opposite: The summer of 1959. Audrey and Mel arrive in London from Zurich. For years the couple lived a peripatetic life, renting around the world depending on where they were working. However, they made their base in Switzerland; first at the Villa Bethania near Bürgenstock, then later at Tolochenaz-sur-Morges above Lake Geneva, where Audrey would live for the rest of her life.

Above: Audrey and Mel epitomized the glamorous, international jet-setting couple. Audrey's greatest desire, however, had always been to have children. Their frequent separations due to work meant it was some time into their marriage before Audrey became pregnant.

Left: A still from *The Unforgiven*, filmed during 1959, co-starring Burt Lancaster and directed by John Huston. It was a grueling production. Audrey was in early pregnancy and fell off her horse while filming.

Opposite: Audrey knits on the set of *The Unforgiven*, perhaps for her unborn child. Audrey was devastated when the child was stillborn. She slid into a deep depression. However, she gave birth to a healthy son the following year. Mel wired a close friend: "AUDREY BEATIFICALLY HAPPY".

Opposite: One of the most famous images of the twentieth century, Audrey as Holly Golightly in one of her most acclaimed films, *Breakfast at Tiffany's*, 1961. Holly is a gold-digging escort, played with so much wit and charm by Audrey that contemporary audiences, who might have been shocked, hardly noticed. Audrey received an Oscar nomination for her performance in the movie, although Sophia Loren won the award for *Two Women*. During her career Audrey was nominated five times by the Academy: *Roman Holiday*, *Sabrina*, *The Nun's Story*, *Breakfast at Tiffany's* and *Wait Until Dark*.

Right: Once again donning an outfit by her style guru, Givenchy, for *Breakfast at Tiffany's*.

Above: With co-star George Peppard in *Breakfast at Tiffany's*. Holly fantasizes about the jewelry in Tiffany's.

Opposite: Audrey with Patricia Neal and George Peppard from a scene in a New York street. The great film-score composer Henry Mancini said, "Audrey's big eyes gave me the push to get a little more sentimental than I usually am. 'Moon River' was written for her. No one else ever understood it so completely." The producers had wanted to cut it from the movie but it is one of the most famous scenes in twentieth-century film.

Above: The actors take a break from filming *Breakfast at Tiffany's* on a busy New York street. In many ways, the film is a love song to New York. The original book by Truman Capote is, in his own words, more "bitter" than the film. He had wanted Marilyn Monroe to play the part of Holly Golightly. Many years later, Audrey described the movie as "the one I feel least uncomfortable watching. But the two things I always think of when I see it are (1) how could I have abandoned my cat? And (2) Truman Capote really wanted Marilyn Monroe for the part."

Opposite: Audrey at a London charity première of *Breakfast at Tiffany's*, 1961. As Audrey's star continued to rise, Mel's began to decline. He even admitted that "it's a problem when the wife outshines the husband as Audrey does me". Audrey wanted to be a support to Mel but it was becoming clear to their close friends that all was not well between them.

Above: Clement Attlee, the former British Prime Minister, talks to Audrey at the premiere.

Opposite: When Audrey came to the public's attention, *Vogue* magazine said of her, "She has so captured the public imagination and the mood of the time that she has established a new standard of beauty, and every other face now approximates to the "Hepburn look" … This slim person, with the winged eyebrows … is the world's darling."

Right: Publicity shot of Audrey with co-stars James Garner and Shirley MacLaine in *The Children's Hour*, 1961. This was a radical departure for Audrey. It was based on Lillian Hellman's play of the same name. MacLaine's and Hepburn's characters are teachers accused by a child of having an affair. Despite a number of its more controversial scenes being cut, many audiences still found the subject matter unpalatable.

Opposite and above: In 1963, a decade after Cary Grant (above) had turned down the part of Linus Larrabee in
Sabrina, he and Audrey starred in *Charade*, a comedy thriller set in France. Although Grant at first believed
himself to be too old to play opposite Audrey, their relationship in the film brims with wit and charm. They liked
and respected each other. Grant gave her a few words of advice that she never forgot: "You've got to like
yourself a little more."

Right and opposite: Just a few days after the filming of *Charade* was completed, Audrey began work on *Paris – When it Sizzles*, a 1963 spoof on Hollywood screenwriters. In this film, Audrey was reunited with her former lover, William Holden. His drinking had become debilitating – to such an extent that production of the film had to be halted. The studio held up the film's release for two years. One of the great draws for Audrey was that Givenchy would once again design her wardrobe.

Opposite: Audrey in 1965. Life was full of conflicts: supporting Mel's career, continuing her own and being a mother. She discovered she was pregnant again this year, but lost the baby. Mel said, "She took it very, very hard."

Right: Richard Attenborough and Audrey at an award ceremony in London. In 1965 Audrey won the Bafta for Best Actress in *Charade* and Attenborough was awarded Best Actor for *Guns at Batasi*. Mel was trying to secure various projects with Audrey's collaboration, which often guaranteed their go-ahead.

Above: Jack L. Warner, head of Warner Bros Studios in Hollywood, with Audrey and Rex Harrison in 1963. Both actors have just signed to star in *My Fair Lady*, directed by George Cukor. The musical, based on George Bernard Shaw's play *Pygmalion*, had opened on Broadway in 1956 and run for over 2500 performances. Contractual complications meant that no film could be made until the end of the London stage run which meant that there had been a great deal of speculation in Hollywood as to who would win the coveted lead roles. Audrey had wanted to take on the part for years. She once said, "I'd do anything to play Eliza Doolittle."

Opposite: Audrey as Eliza Doolittle at Ascot. Cecil Beaton, a long-time fan of Audrey, designed the striking black and white costumes that made this scene one of the most memorable in cinematic history, winning him an Academy Award for Best Costumes.

Opposite: A still during the shooting of an early scene in *My Fair Lady* with Wilfrid Hyde-White (left) and Rex Harrison, standing with a cup and saucer. Throughout the production, Audrey trained very hard to get her voice into shape. However, unknown to her, Marni Nixon was recording most of the songs, which would eventually be dubbed over Audrey's voice. Some critics believe that although Marni Nixon's singing is flawless, Audrey's own voice might have kept closer to the character of Eliza.

Right: Audrey's co-star Rex Harrison won the Oscar for Best Actor for *My Fair Lady* and many thought that Audrey deserved a nomination for her performance in the movie. Ironically, Julie Andrews, who had been in the original stage version, and was overlooked in favor of Audrey for the film role, won an Oscar for *Mary Poppins* which was released in the same year.

Opposite: In *How to Steal a Million*, a sharp crime caper, 1966. Audrey was once again clothed by Givenchy. Here the great designer shows he has wit as well as sophistication.

Right: Audrey with her leading man, Peter O'Toole in *How to Steal a Million*. The production was great fun, according to all who worked on the film, not least because of O'Toole's relaxed manner.

Left: Audrey and Albert Finney relax on the beach during the filming of *Two for the Road*, 1967. They had a short but very happy affair at a time when Audrey's marriage to Mel was increasingly unhappy. The director Stanley Donen noticed: "She was so free, so happy. I never saw her like that ... I guess it was Albie." Audrey had been reluctant to accept the role when Donen had first proposed it, feeling that the project was too avant-guarde for her tastes. However, the movie was praised by critics and both she and Albert Finney received favorable reviews for their performances.

Opposite: Audrey takes a break during the filming of *Two for the Road*.

Above: In the thriller *Wait Until Dark* Audrey played a blind woman whose life was in danger. She worked hard to understand what it would be like to be visually impaired, attending a school for the blind and even learning some Braille. This was a difficult production for Audrey: Mel was the producer, which constrained the artistic freedom she was normally allowed, and she missed her son Sean dreadfully. When she finished filming to return to Switzerland, Audrey said, "It will be a long time before I make another film." She was true to her word, not returning to acting for nearly a decade until taking on the role of Lady Marian opposite Sean Connery in *Robin and Marian*.

Opposite: Audrey with Efrem Zimbalist Jnr, who played her husband in *Wait Until Dark*.

Above: Mel and Audrey separated in the summer of 1967 and the following January, she married Italian psychiatrist and playboy Andrea Dotti, after a whirlwind romance. Audrey had a son, Luca, with Dotti but the marriage was a difficult one, in part because of Dotti's many infidelities. Audrey's son Sean from her first marriage said: "My stepfather was a brilliant and funny psychiatrist – but he was a hound dog. He just didn't know how to be faithful. Not a good choice of husband if what you are looking for is security."

Opposite: Audrey moved to Rome for a short time after she married Andrea but soon returned to Switzerland. She was only too ready to swap Hollywood glamor for motherhood and a burgeoning love of gardening that remained with her for the rest of her life. Here a photographer snaps a rare

Opposite: Audrey and her older son Sean Ferrer attend a tribute to Fred Astaire in Los Angeles, 1981.

Above: In 1980 Audrey met Robert Wolders, a Dutch-born actor who was to be her partner for the rest of her life. She once said, "Ageing doesn't bother me, but loneliness does." Wolders had been married to the film star Merle Oberon, twenty-five years his senior. He was a great support to Audrey, often traveling with her on her UNICEF missions.

Opposite: Audrey attends a UNICEF benefit. In 1988 Audrey began working with UNICEF as a goodwill ambassador. Her love for children, which she had felt since being no more than a child herself, had finally been given more purpose: "I've been given an enormous privilege," she said, "it's to speak for those children who can't speak for themselves. It's an easy task, because children have no enemies. To save a child would be such a blessing." She applied herself to this work with such dedication that it impressed her colleagues at UNICEF. "Giving is living," she once said. "If you stop wanting to give, there's nothing more to live for."

Right: Audrey pictured in 1991.

Left and opposite: With two lifelong friends. Hubert de Givenchy (left), the French designer who dressed Audrey on and off screen, and her first leading man, Gregory Peck (right).

Late in 1992, Audrey was diagnosed with advanced cancer. She died at home at Tolochenaz, surrounded by her beloved sons, Robert Wolders and her two ex-husbands, Mel Ferrer and Andrea Dotti.

FILMOGRAPHY

1948	Nederlands in 7 lessen
	(Dutch in Seven Lessons)
1951	One Wild Oat
	Laughter in Paradise
	Young Wives' Tale
	The Lavender Hill Mob
1952	The Secret People
	Monte Carlo Baby
	Nous irons à Monte Carlo
	(We Will Go to Monte Carlo)
1953	Roman Holiday
1954	Sabrina
1956	War and Peace
1957	Funny Face
	Love in the Afternoon
1959	Green Mansions
	The Nun's Story
1960	The Unforgiven
1961	Breakfast at Tiffany's
	The Children's Hour
1963	Charade
1964	Paris – When it Sizzles
	My Fair Lady
1966	How to Steal a Million
1967	Two for the Road
	Wait Until Dark
1976	Robin and Marian
1979	Bloodline
1981	They All Laughed
1989	Always

Theater and Television

1949	High Button Shoes (musical theater)
	Sauce Tartar (musical theater)
1950	Sauce Piquante (musical theater)
1951	Gigi (theater)
1952	CBS Television Workshop
1954	Ondine (theater)
1957	Mayerling (television – released in theaters in Europe)
1987	Love Among Thieves television movie.
1993	Gardens of the World with Audrey Hepburn (PBS miniser